971.9
BEC

Beckett, Harry.

91208

Yukon

YUKON

JOURNEY ACROSS CANADA

Harry Beckett

The Rourke Book Co., Inc.
Vero Beach, Florida 32964

Harry Beckett M.A. (Cambridge), M.Ed. (Toronto), Dip.Ed. (Hull, England) has taught at the elementary and high school levels in England, Canada, France, and Germany. He has also travelled widely for a tour operator and a major book company.

Edited by Laura Edlund
Laura Edlund received her B.A. in English literature from the University of Toronto and studied Writing for Multimedia and Book Editing and Design at Centennial College. She has been an editor since 1986 and a traveller always.

ACKNOWLEDGMENTS
For photographs: Geovisuals (Kitchener, Ontario), The Canadian Tourism Commission and its photographers.
For reference: *The Canadian Encyclopedia, Encarta 1997, The Canadian Global Almanac, Symbols of Canada. Canadian Heritage*, Reproduced with the permission of the Minister of Public Works and Government Services Canada, 1997.
For maps: Promo-Grafx of Collingwood, Ont., Canada.

Library of Congress Cataloging-in-Publication Data

Beckett, Harry. 1936 -
   Yukon / by Harry Beckett.
     p. cm. — (Journey across Canada)
   Includes index.
   Summary: An introduction to the geography, history, economy,major cities, and interesting sites of Canada's northwestern province made famous by the stories of Jack London and the poetry of Robert Service.
   ISBN 1-55916-208-2
   1. Yukon Territory—Juvenile literature.   [1. Yukon Territory.]
I. Title II. Series: Beckett, Harry, 1936 -   Journey across Canada.
F1091.4.B43 1997
971.9'1—dc21   97–20690
                                                  CIP
                                                  AC

Printed in the USA

TABLE OF CONTENTS

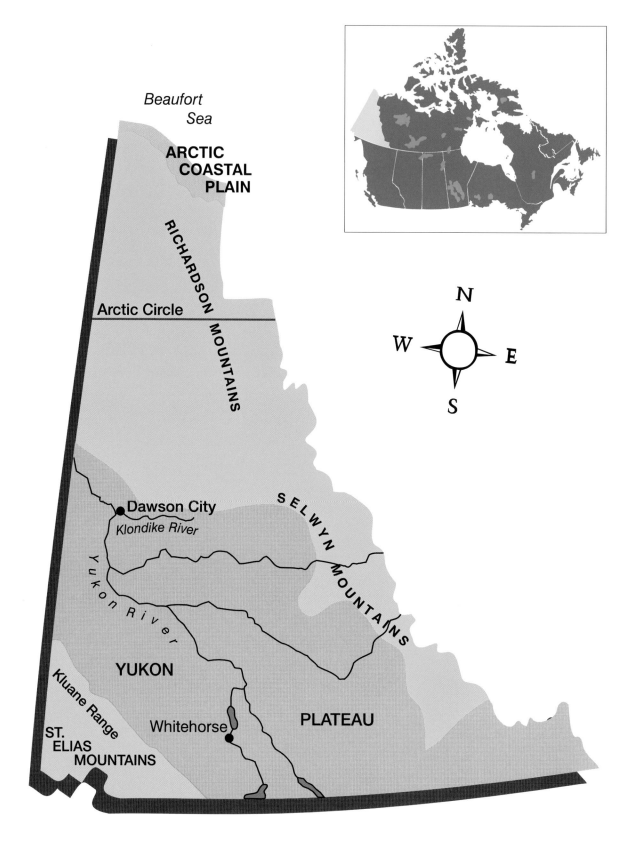

Beaufort
Sea

**ARCTIC
COASTAL
PLAIN**

RICHARDSON MOUNTAINS

Arctic Circle

● Dawson City
Klondike River

Yukon River

S E L W Y N   M O U N T A I N S

YUKON

Kluane Range

ST.
ELIAS
MOUNTAINS

Whitehorse
●

PLATEAU

N
W   E
S

YUKON TERRITORY

Chapter One

SIZE AND LOCATION

Yukon Territory is pie-shaped and lies in the northwest corner of Canada, north of the 60th **parallel** (PER uh lel). Part is north of the **Arctic Circle** (ARK tik SUR kul).

The Yukon is bordered to the west by the state of Alaska, to the south by British Columbia, and to the east by the Northwest Territories. Its northern boundary is the Beaufort Sea, an arm of the Arctic Ocean. Yukon Territory is about 950 kilometres (590 miles) from east to west, and 1100 kilometres (684 miles) from north to south.

In total, the Yukon is 483 450 square kilometres (186 675 square miles) in area, which is about 5% of the Canadian surface.

Find out more...

- There are about 343 kilometres (213 miles) of coastline.
- In 1996 the population was 30 766. Of these people, 58.8% live in towns and cities, and about 14% are Native.

Chapter Two

GEOGRAPHY: LAND AND WATER

The Yukon's main feature is the Yukon Plateau. It is high and rolling, with **isolated** (I suh late ud) mountains and deep valleys cut by the territory's major rivers. Almost two thirds of the water in the territory flow into the Yukon River system. The Yukon's largest lakes are at the southern end of the plateau.

Mount Logan, in the St. Elias Mountains, is the highest mountain in Canada.

A distant view of the Kluane Range

The plateau is bounded to the east by the Richardson and Selwyn Mountains, and to the southwest by the St. Elias Mountains, part of the Coast Mountains of western Canada.

In the north, the Arctic Coastal Plain slopes down to the Beaufort Sea. This area and much of the area to the south, is **permafrost** (PUR muh frost). Any buildings and roads must be built carefully so that the permafrost does not thaw.

Chapter Three

WHAT IS THE WEATHER LIKE?

Cold arctic air has a strong influence on the Yukon's climate. The winters are extremely cold, but the summers are warm or even hot. Sometimes air flows in from the Pacific to warm the winter. Dawson City has only 90 frost-free days annually.

The Yukon is also quite dry because the Coast Mountains shelter the interior from the moisture blown off the Pacific Ocean. Most rain falls between June and August. April is the driest month. Snowfall is light, but it stays on the ground for seven months a year.

Summer days are long and sunny, but winter nights are also long. North of the Arctic Circle, the sun does not set at all during midsummer. However, it does not rise at all during midwinter.

Find out more...

- The difference between summer and winter temperatures is the greatest in North America—40°C (72° F)!
- Whitehorse gets nearly 20 hours of sunlight per day in June.

Dry and clear weather on the sheltered side of the mountains

Chapter Four

Agriculture is a small industry because of the Yukon's soil and climate. People grow food for local use, but good roads now make it easy to truck in what is needed.

Fur trading is the oldest industry and still important to Native peoples, as are hunting and fishing. There is salmon fishing in the Yukon River and the rivers that flow into it. The salmon are dried and smoked using traditional methods. Fish are also caught for local sale and for canning. Some lakes are stocked for sport-fishing.

Three fifths of the land below the **tree line** (TREE line) is forested, but only 15% is useful to the lumber industry.

A lumberman shows his skills at the Discovery Days festival.

Find out more...

- Lynx, martens, wolverine, fox, muskrat, and beaver are all trapped or hunted.
- Caviar (fish eggs) is also canned and exported to Japan.
- Trees grow slowly in the Yukon—10 metres (33 feet) in 100 years.

Chapter Five

Centuries ago, Native peoples settled the area. Among others, there were the **Nahani** (nuh HAH nee) in the east and the **Kutchin** (koo CHIN) along the Yukon River.

Eventually, Europeans came. In 1825, the explorer Sir John Franklin arrived. Traders for the Hudson's Bay Company came in the 1840s, followed by whale hunters.

A Native drawing of an animal symbol

Outside his cabin, poems by the famous Yukon poet Robert Service are read.

In 1896, gold was discovered on Bonanza Creek, which runs into the Klondike River. Newcomers poured into the area. Between 1897 and 1904, gold diggers found about $100 million worth of gold. In 1898, the Yukon was made a territory, with many of the powers of a province.

Since then, other minerals, the building of the Alaska Highway during World War II (1939-45), and tourism have drawn newcomers here.

Chapter Six

MAKING A LIVING: FROM INDUSTRY

Mining makes up over 30% of the Yukon's economy, with some of the world's largest deposits of lead, zinc, silver, and tungsten. There are also gold and many other metallic and non-metallic deposits.

Manufacturing is limited to activities such as milling lumber and refining minerals. The Yukon has enough rivers to generate all the electric power it needs.

Tourism is the Yukon's second most important industry. Stories by Jack London, poems by Robert Service, and reminders of the Klondike Gold Rush draw the tourists. Where before gold seekers came by foot and steamboat, now visitors travel on highways and by airplane.

Find out more...

• The Yukon also has copper, asbestos, oil, and gas.
• Almost 30% of the work force is employed in tourism.

A tourist pans for gold, just as the first prospectors did.

Chapter Seven

IF YOU GO THERE...

Have you seen old pictures of gold seekers climbing in single file over the Chilkoot Pass on their way to the Klondike? Now, summer hikers can make the three- to five-day trek through Gold Rush history.

Visitors can also hunt, fish, canoe, and camp in magnificent scenery. Especially at night, the **aurora borealis** (o ROR uh bor ee AL is) often dances overhead.

Many festivals look forward to the end of winter. The best-known is Whitehorse's Sourdough Rendezvous, a week of dogsled races, cabin building, moose stew, and **bannock** (BAN uk). The Gold Rush is celebrated at Dawson City's Discovery Days, a festival of rafting, canoeing, parades, and dancing. Every six years, the Yukon hosts the Arctic Winter Games.

Moose, Dall sheep, goats, caribou, black bears and grizzly bears roam Kluane Park.

F**ind out more...**

• Each prospector had to take "a ton of goods" over the pass—907 kilograms or 2000 pounds!

• Kluane National Park has ice fields, glaciers, and the country's highest mountains.

Chapter Eight
MAJOR CITIES

Dawson City lies at the junction of the Yukon and Klondike Rivers. After the Bonanza gold discovery of 1896, the population soared to over 30 000, but later decreased. Dawson City became the Yukon's first capital. Now, tourists come for Gold Rush history, wilderness, and Native culture.

Dawson City, with its rivers, seen from Midnight Dome

The main street of Whitehorse

Whitehorse lies on the Yukon River in a protected valley, between mountains and the river. It was a small mining town (of 750 people in 1941), until the coming of the Alaska Highway in 1942. It grew quickly and was made the capital of the Yukon in 1953. The main employers are mining, government, trade, and tourism. The historic steamboat S.S. Klondike, is one of many attractions.

Chapter Nine

SIGNS AND SYMBOLS

The flag's three coloured panels represent the forests, the snow, and the deep blue northern waters. The coat of arms sits on the middle panel, framed by the territorial flower, the fireweed.

The cross of St. George of England on the shield in the coat of arms represents the early British explorers and traders. The circle on the cross symbolizes the fur trade. Below, the blue and white wavy lines represent the Yukon River and the gold-bearing creeks of the Klondike. The red spikes and gold disks represent the mountains and their mineral resources.

The malamute dog, standing on a mound of snow, played a large role in the territory's history. It is known for its loyalty, stamina, and strength.

The fireweed is a summer flower that is the first to appear after a forest fire. Its young sprouts are cooked and eaten as greens.

Yukon's flag, coat of arms, and flower

GLOSSARY

Arctic Circle (ARK tik SUR kul) — a parallel (66°32') north of the equator, above which the sun does not set during midsummer and does not rise during midwinter

aurora borealis (o ROR uh bor ee AL is) — shows of different coloured lights in northern skies; also called "Northern Lights"

bannock (BAN uk) — a flat flour cake

isolate (I suh late) — to separate from others

Kutchin (koo CHIN) — a Native people of central and northern Yukon, and beyond

Nahani (nuh HAH nee) — Native peoples of northeastern Canada, including the Kaska people

parallel (PER uh lel) — a line on a map joining points at the same distance from the equator

permafrost (PUR muh frost) — ground that is always frozen at, or just below, the surface

tree line (TREE line) — a point beyond which trees will not grow because of the climate

In Dawson City, signs of the Gold Rush are everywhere.

INDEX